THE BALVIHAR BOOK OF GURUDEV'S TALES

ILLUSTRATED BY

Bharati Sukhatankar

CENTRAL CHINMAYA MISSION TRUST
MUMBAI - 400 072

First Edition	December	2001	-	3000 copies
Revised Edition	May	2002	-	2000 copies
Reprint	February	2003	-	2000 copies
Reprint	February	2004	-	2000 copies
Reprint	April	2005	-	2000 copies
Reprint	April	2006	-	2000 copies

Published by:

CENTRAL CHINMAYA MISSION TRUST
Sandeepany Sadhanalaya
Saki Vihar Road,
Mumbai - 400 072, INDIA.
Tel: 91-22-28572367 / 28575806
Fax: 91-22-28573065
Email: ccmt@vsnl.com
Website: www.chinmayamission.com

Distribution Centre in USA:

CHINMAYA MISSION WEST
Publications Division,
560 Bridgetown Pike,
Langhorne, PA 19053, USA.
Tel: (215) 396-0390
Fax: (215) 396-9710
Email: publications@chinmaya.org
Website: www.chinmayapublications.org

Printed by

SAGAR UNLIMITED
28-B, Nand-Deep Industrial Estate,
Kondivita Lane, Andheri Kurla Road,
Mumbai-400 059.
Tel.: 28362777 / 28227699

Price: Rs. 55=00

ISBN 81-7597-022-7

Foreword

The Bal Vihar magazine has played a vital role in the history of the Chinmaya Mission. Started in 1969 by Pujya Gurudev Swami Chinmayananda it was aimed at moulding the minds of the children and thereby laying the foundation for producing men and women of strong moral character, upholding the timeless values of Indian culture. Pujya Gurudev's idea was to "catch them young."

Towards this goal, Bal Vihar has worked for over thirty years. Much valuable material has been published so far and so it was decided that in this, the 50th year of the Chinmaya Movement, it would be a good idea to reprint a series of all-colour Bal Vihar books under different titles. This would strengthen the grass root level activities and help the Bal Vihar children and sevaks.

I commend the work done by the Bal Vihar team and wish them all success in their ongoing efforts.

Mumbai

December 2001

(Swami Tejomayanada)

EDITOR'S NOTE

Gurudev's tales were often the highlight of his talks. He always said that Vedantic truths were high and subtle and therefore not within the grasp of all people. So he drew freely upon his vast storehouse of tales to drive home a truth. *"None of these stories that are attributed to me are really mine. They are stories that old Mahatmas told us while we were learning at the feet of the Masters in Utterkashi and Rishikesh",* he said. Retelling these stories for children with profuse colour illustrations is our tribute to this master story - teller, in this, the 50th year of the Chinmaya Movement.

Mumbai

December 2001   (Brni. Vividisa Chaitanya)

INDEX

WHO IS GOD?.......

Once upon a time there was a pious and benevolent king who ruled over Lakshana Kingdom with the help of his most faithful Chief Minister, Satyavrita, who was equally pious and a highly intelligent statesman. The people respected their King, but loved and adored their Chief Minister.

Time passed on. In the palace, satsangs were conducted daily by great saints and sages, poets and pundits. The old King and the Minister frequently discussed the scriptural declarations regarding the Science of Reality. The King had a son who often was present at their discussions, but the young prince could not follow them. He was too young and was totally uninitiated.

The old King died. Long live the King! The young prince was duly installed on the throne. The aged Minister continued serving the throne, and deep within himself the young King felt a filial reverence towards the noble Chief Minister. And yet, when the Minister used terms like God, His grace, His blessing, His glory, in his talks and discussions, the King got impatient. In the beginning he kept his irritation well hidden. But as time passed, it started showing and one day he burst out with irresistable vehemence.

When long suppressed irritations burst out, the floods are usually annihilating and devastating.

"Look here, Sir", thundered the young King. "Out of respect for you and the memory of my father I have kept quiet for so long. You talk of God and His Grace. I don't understand it at all. When I discuss this topic with others, they make some vague statements, and mention some unscientific conclusions. Shamelessly they argue illogically to reach a blind alley of self-contradictions. I think it is all unprofitable and dangerous superstition. And unless I myself am convinced of it, I will be untrue to my crown if I recognise and encourage such meaningless superstition in my kingdom. Therefore I give you, Sir, 41 days to bring me the answer to these three questions:

Who is God?

Where is He? and

What does He do?

Convince me with your answers and then I will be with you all the way. But if I am not convinced, then I shall guide my kingdom into a purely materialistic life and initiate atheism as our royal policy. I believe in intellectual honesty. I cannot be dishonest to myself."

The old Minister smiled in dignified silence and walked out. His prayerful anxiety was, "Oh Lord! Give me the right power of expression to communicate a glimpse of Thy glory to this young boy's noble heart."

The aged Minister started visiting sages and saints, monasteries, ashrams, colleges of theology, schools of philosophical studies and institutes of mysticism. He discussed with pundits, acharyas, aged brahmins, learned householders. Everywhere he heard more or less the same type of answers, the same quotations from the Upanishads, the Puranas, and other Shastras. All confirmed what he already knew, but none of them could possibly ignite faith in the doubting heart of the young King. Nothing that he heard could initiate a conviction in the rational bosom of the young boy.

Time was running out. The entire Capital had heard of the command of their young King. Everyone was anxious for the revered Minister to find the solution. The old man silently prayed to the Lord to  save his old King's son and the kingdom. He undertook long pilgrimages, and went for short trips, to visit the wise men and the masters. Nowhere could he get any direct guidance; no immediate help came.

The Minister had a faithful old cook who watched the thoughtful worried, anxious face of his master, Satyavrita.

The aged Minister was not eating well; he had grown careless of his dress. Not that he was in despair, but he was becoming worried for the future of the country.

The forty-first day dawned. The entire Capital was expectant of what would happen the following day. Surely, the far-sighted Minister would resign if he failed to satisfy the royal whim.

That evening too, the Minister returned home after his last few, futile, visits to mahatmas, and fruitless discussions with pundits. Despair was writ large on his face. The cook saw this. He approached his master and said, "Sir, during my thirty years of service in this house, I have never seen you so unhappy as you are now. I wish I could help you."

The Minister said, "No one can give conviction to anyone else; that is the truth. The Lord alone can give it to the young King. And He will do it, I know. But how? My despair is at my own impatience to understand His plan."

The cook said nothing.

Next day the darbar hall was full. The people had closed their shops and business houses and, in a grim mood of expectancy had crowded everywhere around in the hall. The King arrived and took his seat on his throne. The Chief Minister's seat was ominously vacant. All other ministers were in their seats earlier than usual.

There was a melancholic silence in the hall. The King in his royal splendour felt the unusual atmosphere and looked around. Suddenly, they saw a man enter by the main door and come forward. The soldiers stopped him on his path, a whispered talk –

and they moved and made way for him.

Approaching the King, the man said, "Long live the King! I am here on behalf of the Chief Minister. He has sent me here to answer your spiritual questions."

The announcement brought relief to everyone. Thrilled expectations rose in their hearts. The King impatiently said, "Alright then. Let's start. Who is God?"

The man smiled and answered, "I am a loyal subject and you are my King. You can command me. But I cannot teach you the Science of Reality, the spiritual wisdom, unless you accept the position of a disciple. A guru can initiate only his disciple."

The young King had been constantly brooding over this mysterious problem all these six weeks, and

so had grown extremely thirsty to know. Therefore, the honest student in the King got up and with folded palms said, "Revered pundit, please accept me as a disciple and teach me."

Without the least hesitation, the man walked straight to the throne and sat on it. Then he commanded the young King to sit down in front of him. Addressing the King he said, "What is your first question?"

The King in all humility now repeated, "Who is God?"

The man smiled and looked around the hall. All faces were eagerly awaiting the answer. Instead of immediately replying, he called an attendant and ordered him to bring to the hall the black milching cow from the palace cowshed. In a short time the cow was brought. The man asked one of them to milk the cow. The freshly drawn milk was brought to him in a golden bowl. He looked into it and passed it on to the young King.

In wonder the King received it. There was a solid and perceptible silence, pierced with a voiceless expectancy hanging all over the hall and outside in the courtyard.

The man's voice rang out in the silence. "Do you see, O Rajan, the milk in the bowl?"

"Yes, Sir."

"What is its colour?"

"Sir, it is pure white."

"What is the colour of the cow that gave this white milk?"

"Black, Sir."

"What does the cow eat to produce milk?"

"Grass, Sir."

"And what is the colour of the grass?"

"Green, Sir."

"And who converts the green grass, in a black cow, into white milk? Can any one do this? Have you any minister-in-charge who can take up a programme of making white milk from green grass in a black cow?"

There was silence. The man, after a meaningful pause, said, "My friends! The power that converts green grass into white milk in a black cow – that is God."

A wave of murmurs and whispered talks followed. Evidently all understood. The King smiled in gratitude and asked, "Sir, please tell me now, where is God? You alone can explain it to me."

Again the man called one of the officers and whispered to him some instructions. In a short time a gold plate with a candle and a match box on it was brought. At a sign from the pundit, soldiers closed all the doors and windows of the hall. There was pitch darkness within. The man struck a match and lit the candle. In the light of the dancing flame, he said, "Till now we were in darkness. The light of the candle has removed the darkness as you all see here. Now tell me, Rajan, where is the light of the candle – not the flame – I am asking where exactly is the light of the candle?"

The King immediately answered, "The light is everywhere."

The man smiled and said, "God is everywhere, as the light of the candle is everywhere in the hall now."

The man clapped his hands together and immediately all doors and windows were opened. Daylight flooded in.

The King was evidently satisfied. He said, "Panditji, please explain to me, "What does God do?"

"That is easy to explain," said the man. At that very moment, he saw the Chief Minister coming down the corridor, head bent in despair. He entered the hall gravely and without looking right or left , he walked straight to his seat, bowed and saluted the throne as usual, and took his seat. His heart had but one prayer, "Lord, help the young King. He is the noble son of a great man, and it is my last responsibility that I guide him to faith. He is capable of running the country on our cultural values, but he needs to be convinced. And I can't give him faith. I have not the ability to carry conviction to his heart. You alone can bless him."

In the enfolding silence the man said, "Rajan if you have understood, "Who is God," and "Where He is," then it is unnecessary for you to ask, "What does He do?" Everything happening in this universe is His doing, executed through the names and forms in the world."

The energetic heart of the youthful King could not appreciate this answer. The audience carried a blank look on their faces. The man sighed and said, "Rajan. See where you are now sitting? Look at our revered Minister – struck with wonder at seeing his stupid old cook in your seat – see where I am sitting – on the throne of the Lakshana Kingdom! He who brings about these ups and downs, including the new uderstanding and wisdom that you are gaining – all are done by Him alone."

There was a thunderous applause in which even the King joined. When the ovation was over, the cook got up from the golden throne, walked up to the Chief Minister, now smiling benignly, and prostrated. "Sir, it was all due to your grace that I was able to answer the King and satisfy him this morning. You were over anxious to serve the King and so felt incompetent to answer him. A doctor, however great he may be, cannot confidently perform even a minor surgery upon his only son."

Through the continued ovation, with bowed head, humbly acknowledging the satisfaction and joy of the assembled ministers and officials, the cook went out.

The King touched the feet of the faithful, revered Minister and taking the royal chain with its emerald pendant from his neck, in the presence of all, he put it around the neck of the Chief Minister.

By now the crowd outside had heard what had happened within the hall. They raised their cry of joy, "Maharaj-ki-jai!" The King went out to the balcony to receive the greetings of his faithful people.

GOD PLUS ME

Nandu had just completed his education and looked forward to starting a new phase in life. His father and mother were parents of modest means and Nandu felt happy that at last, he would be able to contribute towards household expenses. With hope in his heart and a song on his lips, he set out to look for a job.

He asked his friends and acquaintances, he applied to offices and companies, he knocked the doors of schools and colleges. Sorry, so sorry, there was no vacancy. Days passed into weeks and the weeks dragged their feet into months. But there was no job for Nandu.

Despairing and despondent, Nandu went to visit Babaji, a well - known saint who lived on the outskirts of the village. "Please help me, Babaji," he said approaching the holy man with respect and humility.

"My dear boy," said Babaji, "how can I help you procure a job? I neither run a school nor a factory. Neither a company nor a business. All I have is this piece of land. This you can have, for today I

leave on a pilgrimage and it might be some months before I return."

Nandu looked at Babaji's smiling face and outstretched hands. He saw land that was dry and rocky. Land that was cracked and parched for want of water.

"Well?" asked Babaji, "Will you take it?"

Nandu tried not to show his disappointment. He swallowed hard, bit his lip and in a low voice muttered, "I'll take it."

"Good," said Babaji and went his way.

"Well," thought Nandu. "Here I am, landed with a piece of land which has never seen the blessing of a running stream of water. Which has never produced anything save the short-lived weeds that the monsoon rain brings. Well, I've really landed myself with something, haven't I ?"

He rose early the next morning and went to the bazaar. He invested in a pick-axe, a shovel, a hoe. Then he went to his land, pulled his dhoti up above his knees and set to work.

O, it was hard work, mind you. Digging a well. Loosening the soil and rocks, preparing the soil for planting. Buying good quality seeds. Planting them evenly, watering them every day. Uprooting weeds. But Nandu did it. If yellow and brown dry land is all that life has to offer, he thought, why, I have the ability to turn it lush and green.

The days and weeks and months sped by on winged feet. Nandu hardly noticed the passage of time, so busy was he with his new-found farming till one day, as he stood back to admire his green millet crop, he heard a deep, sonorous voice, "Hari Om! Hari Om!" He turned to see Babaji standing before him.

"What is this I see ?" exclaimed Babaji. "What a miracle! what a transformation! who would have believed this to be the same piece of infertile barren land that I gave you? The Lord be praised. It is all His glory, isn't it?"

"Just a minute Babaji," said Nandu. "God's glory, certainly. But my hard work as well. You saw, didn't you, the state of this land when it was just the Lord's glory manifesting? And the difference made by my hard work?"

"You are right," said Babaji. "We should not expect God to do everything for us. What a difference it makes when we help Him out a bit!"

THE CLEVER BANDICOOT

It was soon after the first few, heavy showers of the rainy season. The grasses had grown tall, and the entire world all around seemed to have washed and dressed itself fresh in golden green. The gardens had revived.

Sri Bandicoot, who was living with his happy family near a big vegetable farm, contented with himself, fat and heavy, stretched himself and watched the bright sun streaming down through the clouds. The rains had at last stopped. Sri Bandicoot thought, "I will just run up along the hedges and inspect how my farm garden is flourishing".

He inspected the vegetable beds, the potatoes, the onion and garlic bulbs, the cauliflowers, the tomatoes, the fruits, apples, limes, oranges - he was more than satisfied. Whistling to himself, he was returning when he saw his friend, Sri Donkey, head down, lost in his own thoughts, going in the opposite direction.

"Good morning! Where are you going?" enquired Bandicoot. "Good morning! Why do you want to know? If you want to know, I can tell you, I am going to look at my farm. Normally, now and then at night, I visit it."

"Yes, yes. I have seen it very often. As soon as you get there, the farmer is also there... and what you get from him! Tell me, are they as painful as the sound indicates? They sound like heavy blows!"

"No , No , my friend. You don't know. I am experienced in receiving such blows all day, and so when I get a few in the night for the privilege of grazing in the garden, I don't mind them at all!"

Sri Bandicoot, still laughing, said, "My bow-legs are stronger than your long hind legs. They cannot take you as fast as mine can - no farmer can ever get at me with his stick."

"What do you say? Your tiny dandy legs are stronger than my steel-like strong hind legs! You are a fool."

"All right. Let us have a bet," boasted Sri Bandicoot. "Let us have a test run. He who wins shall have exclusive rights over the vegetable garden. The loser must accept starvation to death."

The suggestion was acceptable to Sri Donkey. It was settled that in half an hour's time they would both meet in the school playground and run from one end to the other of the foot-ball grounds. "That should decide who has stronger legs," said Sri Donkey, and he felt so happy that he frisked about, braying hoarsely, "AHAI-KYA! HAI-KYA! KHUDA! HAI! HAI! KHUDA-HAI!"

This was a matter of life and death. Sri Bandicoot did some hard thinking. Then he ran home, called out to his wife and said, "Get ready quickly. We are both going to the school playground. Right now. I have challenged Sri Donkey for a race. He who wins will have the exclusive rights to the vegetable farm down the street. The loser will die of starvation."

The poor lady was aghast. She began to despair. She could not believe that her wise husband had so foolishly made such a  bad bet. "Be quiet!" he said. "You females should not interfere with us males. You just come with me."

As a dutiful Bharatiya-lady-rat, she quickly got ready and they both started.

They carefully ran and crossed the street, and safely reached the play-ground. As they were crossing the play-ground, Sri Bandicoot whispered to his wife, "Look, darling. You can help me now. You stay at this end. When Sri Donkey runs and reaches here, just peep out of this hole and say, "I'm here," and go back into the hole. You understand? Again, when you hear the sound of the pounding hoofs of Sri Donkey, bring your head out and again say, "I am here". That is all. Will you do this for me?" Smt. Bandicoot felt very cross and terribly unhappy that her husband should ask such a question. "When have I not obeyed your wishes? Why do you ask me, "Will you?" Certainly I will do anything for you, my Lord. But I warn you -

 don't try to run against Sri Donkey. He has such long legs, and they are powerful... Please think for a moment - how can you win a race, when we Bandicoots have such a big body and such small legs?"

Sri Bandicoot smiled in satisfaction and said, "You females. If legs are short, still we can win the race because of the strength of the head. You watch, old lady, and tell me what you have to say when we return home victorious." She smiled, as only cultured lady-Bandicoots can!

By this time Sri Donkey had walked on to the play-field. Sri Bandicoot ran and met his adversary there. They decided to start from the end where Sri Donkey was, run to the goal-post at the farthest end, stop, turn, and run back. They both stood. Sri Donkey cried, "Get set, Ready, Go!" and Sri Bandicoot ran. Sri Donkey galloped away with frantic speed, sure of success when he reached the other end. But once there, out of a hole came the head of the Bandicoot. "I am here," it said and disappeared.

Sri Donkey, wondering how this was possible, turned and ran back again, and when he reached the starting point, Sri Bandicoot was standing there, crying out, "I am already here!"

Poor Sri Donkey was worried. He was confused. But he got an idea. "I think you won this race because it was such a short run. Let us run now, ten times, non-stop, goal-post to goal-post across the foot-ball field." Sri Bandicoot hesitated. But the more Sri Bandicoot hesitated, the more confident Sri Donkey became that he would certainly win. At last the challenge was accepted.

They both stood at the starting line, and this time Sri Bandicoot cried, "Get set, Ready, Go!" And off Sri Donkey ran. When he reached the other end, Smt. Bandicoot said, "I am here", and when the Donkey reached the starting end, Sri Bandicoot said, "I am here". The Donkey ran faster and faster each time, and each time at each end he found that Sri Bandicoot was already there saying, "I am here." Faster and faster Sri Donkey ran, and more and more exhausted he became. His tired legs began missing their steps. Once or twice he stumbled. But he regained his balance. And again he ran. He ran faster. His front legs became stiff with weariness and finally he crashed down. In the great speed of its rush, the fall broke his neck and poor Sri Donkey died on the spot.

Sri Bandicoot ran across the field, collected Smt. Bandicoot and both of them returned home

happily. On the way, Smt. Bandicoot stopped and said, "Lord, you are most inconsiderate. That Donkey died and you did not even stop to lift him and bury him." Sri Bandicoot again reminded her that she should leave all such things to the wisdom of her husband.

"Do you think I did not consider all these things? When Sri Donkey was madly running across the football field, the keeper of the field was watching from the school corridor. There, see! He is running towards the dead animal. Surely he will see to the burial of the dead Donkey. You come with me and give me something nice to eat."

"Why should you feel hungry, when you did nothing at all to win the bet?"

"What? Do you think one needs no food to think so hard and with wisdom win over the physical strength of others around us? As soon as you reach home, give me plenty to eat. If you have nothing at home, run across and get some fresh and juicy cabbages from our vegetable garden. Now we are the sole owners of it."

LISTEN, LISTEN, LISTEN TO ME

It was early morning. A Rishi had just finished his worship on the banks of the Ganga, and was wending his way back to his hut.

As he was going, he saw a hunter approaching him from the opposite direction. He had a huge net on his back which was full of twittering birds he had captured. Now the Rishi felt pity for these poor birds. The hunter, when he saw the Mahatma, prostrated. The Mahatma took this opportunity. He sat down on a stone and said.

"My good man, leave these innocent creatures. They belong to the air. Do something else."

So the hunter took the advice of the Mahatma and set the birds free. "Right," he said. "I will go and spear some fish."

"Oh no! no! Don't do that," the Rishi said. "The fish belong to the water. Let them be."

"Well then what should I do?" asked the hunter.

"I have got to do something. I have been just catching birds and spearing fish all my life and my father did it before me and his father before him. Why, I don't know any other work."

"I will tell you what. You go and cut some wood and sell it in the market."

So the hunter prostrated and accepted what the Mahatma said and started his new life.

Every morning he would get up, go into the forest, chop some trees and sell the wood in the market. He did this for some days. Then he thought, "I am doing a better job now. My guru has shown me the right way. I must go and spread this knowledge."

He went into the forest and captured three parrots. He gave them Shiksha and made them learn the following rhyme –

"Parrots, parrots, parrots, all
Listen, listen, listen to me.
The hunter will come
He will spread his net
He will scatter his seeds
He will sing his song.
But parrots, parrots, parrots, all
You must not fall
Into this trap."

The parrots learnt it up perfectly. They then flew up to the trees and started repeating the Shiksha.

"Parrots, parrots, parrots, all
Listen, listen, listen to me..."

The other birds of the trees learnt it too. Soon the parrots of the other trees heard it and they too, picked it up. Before long, all the trees of the forest were full of parrots who kept up this chorus of

"Parrots, parrots, parrots, all
Listen, listen, listen to me..."

And since there was no hunter, they multiplied in number. They ate the fruits and flew from one branch to another and chanted the Shiksha all the time.

Meanwhile, in the next valley there lived another hunter. And as he caught birds every day, there came a time when there was scarcely a bird

left on the trees. And he thought, "Now what happens to me? I have got to live. And I can't do so unless I catch some birds."

So one day, he slung his net across his shoulder and came to this forest. Oh, and he was so happy when he saw the tree above him was full of birds and the next tree and the next and the next. This is too wonderful, he thought. "Narayana has solved my problem for me. Why, I can live in this forest very comfortably." And he looked around him in sheer joy and delight till he heard what all the parrots were chanting –

"Parrots, parrots, parrots all
Listen, listen, listen to me ..."

He thought to himself, "Oh no! This will never do. I will never catch any birds if this is what they keep chanting." The noise became deafening now. Every parrot was repeating –

" ... The hunter will come
He will spread his net
He will scatter his seeds
He will sing his song..."

And the first thing the hunter felt like doing was getting away from it all.

So he went to the Ganges banks and took a wash in the cool, refreshing water. Then he went to the edge of the forest, spread his net, scattered the seeds and lay down under the tree, for he felt he needed some rest.

He must have closed his eyes for just 10 minutes or so, when an unwelcome, familiar twittering and chattering started –

"... But parrots, parrots, parrots all you must not fall into this trap.."

"Oh no! he thought. "Can't these wretched birds leave me in peace?" And muttering a curse, he looked up. But there were no birds. He looked into the next tree. No birds. And the next. Still no birds. Then he looked down and on the ground, in the net, picking at the grains were thousands of these birds repeating all the time, "Parrots, parrots, parrots all..."

"This is it!" The hunter jumped up with an alacrity born of practice and slowly, slowly pulled the string of the net till the net closed up trapping in all the birds.

He slung the net, now heavy with weight, across his back and whistling a gay tune, made for home.

As he was passing through the forest, the hunter who had taught the birds the song cheered up, for he heard thousands of birds chattering –

> "Parrots, parrots, parrots all
> Listen, listen, listen to me ..."

"Ah", he said. "They are clever birds. Look how fast they've picked it up".

But then through the clearing he saw the hunter passing by with a net-load of captured parrots who kept up a steady chorus, "The hunter will come ..." And then he saw the Rishi coming back from his worship on the Ganges banks. They both saw the captured birds chorusing –

> "Parrots, parrots, parrots all ..."

The Rishi looked at his disciple and smiled. The disciple looked back and smiled. Swami Tapovanji smiled. Chinmaya looked and smiled back.

The hunter would come again the next day and capture more birds. And the birds in the net would forever chant—

"Parrots, parrots, parrots, all
Listen, listen, listen to me.
The hunter will come
He will spread his net
He will scatter his seeds
He will sing his song.
But parrots, parrots, parrots, all
You must not fall
Into this trap."

MIND THE GENIE

In a certain hamlet lived a poor but pious man called Narayan Das. He spent much of his time in worshipping the Lord and in serving the religious needs of the community. But as is sometimes the fate of many good people, he remained poor.

Times became harder still when once the crops failed and the village was hit by famine. Narayan Das, however, continued his routine but once in a while wondered how long would life's bitter test go on.

One day, as he sat tired and exhausted, hunger gnawing at his vitals, a thought suddenly came to him. "Why didn't I think of it before? My teacher, I must go to him. He will surely be able to help me."

Narayan Das' teacher lived deep in a forest, far from the village. It took the good man almost a full day's trudging in the hot sun, before he reached his teacher's hut. With bruised feet and mind, he prostrated to the holy man.

"Narayan! After so many years! What brings you such a long way into the forest, my son?"

"Guruji," said Narayan Das respectfully. "I am in deep trouble." And he explained in detail the ravages caused by the famine and the hardships faced by the villagers. "With your wisdom and compassion, Guruji, tell us what we can do to overcome our troubles."

The holy man thought for a moment. "Narayan Das has always been a good, compassionate human being, helpful to man and beast alike. Surely now is the time to reward him for his virtuous deeds." Aloud he said, "Narayan Das. Listen carefully. I will give to you a powerful mantra. When you chant it with devotion and sincerity, it will produce for you a genie, who will do your bidding and fulfil every wish of yours. Use him well, also for the service of others. May you and all in your village see prosperity and plenty once more."

Narayan Das touched the feet of his Master and with a great feeling of blessedness, returned to his village.

Neatening up his little room, he lit an agarbatti and composed his mind to chant the mantra. After several minutes of intense concentration, he felt a presence and heard a gruff voice saying, "Salutations, Master. What is your bidding? Say, and it shall be done." Narayan Das was amazed to see the creature before him. Bald and pot - bellied with gold hoops in his ears, the genie had materialised as if

from thin air.

"Food," thought Narayan Das. "No one in the village has had a decent meal for days. So please arrange a feast that all the villagers may eat well."

No sooner said than done. That day the villagers ate as never before. Second and third helpings of rich food and a variety of sweetmeats. The men thumped each other heartily, the women smiled, the children ate with shouts of glee and the old folk grunted with satisfaction.

"Right, Master," said the genie, "Now what is your bidding?"

"Why don't you rest a while?" said Narayan Das. "We'll think tomorrow about what next is to be done."

"That's not the way I work, Master. I must have work every single minute of the day. If you can't give me that kind of work, why, I will simply eat you up."

Narayan Das gulped. "Okay," he said hastily. "Please repair this hut of mine." In a jiffy, as if by magic, a beautiful little cottage stood in place of the shabby hut. "Next," said the genie. Narayan Das panicked. "How about a nice garden in front?" And before he could blink his

eyes, there before him was a lovely little garden with roses and lilies and marigolds, full of fragance and colour. "Now?" asked the genie.

"Help, help," cried Narayan Das. As fast as his legs would carry him, Narayan Das ran all the way to the forest where his teacher lived, closely followed by the eager genie. He felt a surge of hope when he saw the face of his Master. "Help me. Please help me, before this monster eats me up," he pleaded.

The Master bade the genie stop. To Narayan Das he said," Go back home and fix a large bamboo pole in your courtyard. Instruct the genie to go up and down the pole at all times. When you have any work to be done, summon him and set him to task. Once your work is done, send him back to the pole. That is the only way to control him. Go now and grow in wisdom."

Narayan Das came back home, a greatly relieved man. The genie was given a fat, shiny bamboo pole to slither up and down upon. Over a period of time, Narayan Das achieved much. The prosperity of the village was restored and many new schemes initiated for the welfare of the community. Everyone basked in the glow of peace and progress. But happiest of all was the genie, for he alway had something to do.

Take care. Your mind is the genie. When it is invoked properly, it accomphishes great things in life. When it is idle, it can get up to mischief and even destroy you completely. The bamboo pole is the Lord's name. When the mind is idle send it up and down this pole. When there is work to be done, use it well. Do not allow it to fling you around the regrets of the past, the anxieties of the future or the excitements of the present.

THE LORD OF LOVE

Long, long ago in Arabia, there lived a very pious old man who was a great devotee and lover of God and men. He served all with love in the name of God. All over Arabia his name bacame renowned for piety and hospitality.

One night, when all the servants had gone to sleep and the whole family too was fast asleep, someone knocked at the door. The Arab was awakened by the loud knocks and opened the door. At the door stood an old, unkempt man looking very, very exhausted and famished. He beseeched, "Can you give me some food, sir? I have been starving for the past one week."

The Arab's heart melted at the plight of the old man. He invited him in with great love, gave him a seat and went in. The servants and his family members had been working till late in the evening and were all tired. The Arab did not want to disturb them at that late hour to prepare food for the guest. So he himself went into the kitchen, prepared some food quickly and brought it on a tray into the hall. He placed the food in front of the old man and said, "Sir

 please accept my hospitality in the name of the Lord and bless me. May the Lord be praised!"

The hungry old man dragged the plate nearer and at once started eating the food. In between mouthfuls he said, "Thank you for the food. But why "in the name of the Lord?" Which Lord is there to be worshipped? It is all nonsense."

The Arab was stunned. He had never imagined that there could ever be a man who denied God. "Don't you see, sir, how the kind Lord provided food for you at this late hour in a stranger's house? Could you have survived had not the loving God sustained you throughout your life?"

The old man was busy eating. Still munching he replied. "My dear sir, why do you speak of God? Have you ever seen Him? It is your good nature that made you give me food. I am grateful to you. I am not silly to waste my time thinking of a non-existing God."

This was too much for the Arab. He could no longer contain himself. He burst out in anger, "So you don't believe in God! You feel that you can look after yourself without God! If that is so, get out of my house. There is no place here for atheists." In anger he took away the plate of food from the old man, pushed him out of the house and closed his door. Burning with indignation, he went to bed, prayed to the Lord and fell asleep.

Then the Lord appeared to the Arab in a dream and asked, " Son, why did you push away the poor man before he had finished his meal? He was very hungry. Why did you not allow him to eat his fill?"

The Arab trembled before the Almighty Lord and said, "Oh Lord, I was prepared to give as much food as he wanted. But when he denied You again and

again it was difficult for me to tolerate him. How could I bear his denial of You?"

The Lord smiled and said, "Son he has been denying Me for the last sixty years. Even then I gave him food and sustained him all these years. Could you not tolerate him for even one day for My sake?"

The Arab's head hung in shame. Shedding tears of remorse he prostrated to the Lord and said, "You are the Lord of Love. I know now how kind You are in tolerating all our mistakes, yet giving us all that we need. My Lord let me have the same love for all the beings in the world. Let me not be angry with any one for any reason. Please pardon me for this lapse."

The Lord blessed the Arab and disappeared.

NOTHING BUT SUGAR

Jaggu was a hard working man, who toiled diligently to make a living. By God's grace, he had a dutiful wife and four lovely children. He loved his family dearly and cared for his wife and children, meeting their demands with infinite love and patience.

One day, a mela (travelling fair) came to town. Jaggu saw the huge hoarding advertising the mela on his way home from work. As he passed the Exhibition Grounds, he saw the flurried activity that went into setting up the various stalls for eating and entertainment — the ferris wheel, the merry-go-round and the roller-coaster. "The children will enjoy this," he thought, as he imagined the look of pleasure on their young faces.

"Have you been good children today ?" he asked his children as he kicked off his chappals and settled down to enjoy the hot tea that his wife brought for

 him. "Yes Papa," Yes Papa," they crowded eagerly round their father. "In that case," said Jaggu, pausing for effect. Wide-eyed, the children waited to hear what he would say next. "In that case, coming Saturday, I'll take you all to the mela." "Yea!" the

kids cried excitedly and rushed out to play. Jaggu's wife smiled quietly. What a good father he was. And a good husband too. She was sure he would buy her some new bangles at the fair. She took the empty cup and went back to the kitchen.

Fresh load of work arrived in the office. That whole week Jaggu became totally absorbed in files, records, vouchers, ledgers and receipts. So much so, that he clean forgot his promise to the children. So when he went home on Saturday, he was surprised to see his four kids all spruced up in clean, fresh clothes, his wife in her second best outfit, smiling shyly, with extra kajal in her eyes. "What is all this?" asked Jaggu. "Where are you all going?" "O, to the mela, Papa." "You promised to take us."

For a moment it occured to Jaggu to say that he was too tired, he would take them another day. Then he looked at their bright, eager faces and noticed the slight anxiety that crossed his wife's face. "Okay," he sighed. "Let me freshen up, then we'll go."

The mela was good fun. The children ran across the vast green Exhibition Grounds. Now they were up on the ferris wheel, now driving the bumper-to bumper cars. Now becoming dizzy on the merry-go-round, now trying their luck at shoot-the-duck. Now chasing the balloon wallah, now going for a camel ride.

As they came back to Jaggu, a little tired but their eyes seeking new excitement, a sweet vendor, seeing such a gaggle of children, parked himself nearby. "Sweets, sweets," clamoured the kids. "Papa, please buy us some sweets." "This should be their last treat," said Jaggu to himself, mentally calculating that after buying them sweets, he would have just enough money left for their bus fare back home. And so the kids got their sweets, in multi colours and multi shapes—pink, green, yellow, white, tigers, lions, monkeys, cats and birds – there was much to choose from.

As he counted out the coins and paid the vendor, Jaggu felt happy. It would be some months before he would have to treat the children again or buy new bangles for his wife. However, his happy thoughts were soon interrupted. An unholy quarrel had risen among the children. "My lion," said the eldest "is the king of the jungle. He will make mince meat of your weak little animals."

"No, no," cried the next. "My elephant is strong and powerful. He will trample your lion to death." "Shut up," said the third. "Is the lion or the elephant as clever as the monkey?" "Hoo, hoo," wailed the youngest. "I have only a cat. Not fair, not fair." Jaggu saw a crisis situation. He knew he had to act, and act quickly. Before the children came to blows, he intervened. "Just a minute. Just a minute," he said. "Before we put it to vote as to whose animal is the best, why don't you all put the animals in your

mouth?" The children did as they were told. As their tongues sucked on the sweets and their taste buds revelled in the juicy, sugary taste, they became silent. "Now then, each of you, what is the taste on your tongue? Is the lion bitter, the elephant sour, the monkey chilli-hot, the cat sweet?"

"No," mumbled the children, slurping in between on the sweets.

"They are sweet." "All sweet."

"There you are," said Jaggu smugly, with a note if triumph in his voice. "The essence of sugar is sweetness. Don't focus on the differences which are superficial, any way. Focus on the essence which is common to all."

Just then, the bus taking them home trundled along. Jaggu bundled his tired but happy brood into the bus. His wife settled herself at a window and admired her beautiful new bangles as they caught the glow of the setting sun.

JUST REWARDS

One day a Sadhu was walking along the road. He always dressed in simple clothes, serving all the people who were good, and leading the bad ones to the nobler ways of living through love and service. As he was thus walking in the gathering dusk, he saw a big bungalow. Thinking that it must be a rich man's house and hoping to get some food and a night's rest there, he knocked at the door, "Hari Om, Hari Om", he said.

"Who is that?" barked Kanakapal, the master of the house from an upstairs window. "Hari Om, Hari Om, Hari Om", repeated the Sadhu. "Could you not come in the day-time? Where were you all this time? In the night we don't entertain anyone, Chale jao,"

and the window was closed with a bang. The Sadhu smiled and cheerfully walked away.

Not far away from the arrogant rich man's bungalow was a poor man's humble hut. The Sadhu reached his door and knocked. "Hari Om, Hari Om, Hari Om." The man, Premchand, and his wife came together to open the door and seeing that it was a simple poor devotee of the Lord, they invited him in. The lady immediately went and brought all the food that was there in the house. "We are very sorry. We just finished our dinner. This is all we have now. But it should be sufficient as we also have some milk for you." The Sadhu smiled and joyfully accepted the food.

The woman said, "Let us this night lie on the mat in the front room, and give the Sadhu our bed." Premchand was only too happy to be able to serve his honoured guest.

Before going to bed, they all sat together and talked of the glories of the Lord for more than an hour. The lady then brought milk for the guest and showed him his bed. The Sadhu was very happy to see the couple so devoted and kind.

 Early next morning, the Sadhu finished his daily meditation and prayers, and when he came out of his room he saw the lady was already in the kitchen cooking a frugal breakfast for the guest to eat before he left. The Sadhu could not any longer keep his happiness to himself. He called Premchand near him and said, "I am extremely happy with you both. Now you ask of me three boons."

Premchand said, "The Lord has given us every thing. What more can we ask for? Let us both be healthy and let us serve others till our last day. Let there be enough for us both to live on and a little to share with other needy ones, who might come to us. I don't know anything else that I can ask of you with the third boon."

The Sadhu smiled, and said, "Perhaps you would like to have a better and more comfortable house." Both Premchand and his wife bowed their heads in acceptance.

"Hari Om, Hari Om, Hari Om," the Sadhu took leave of them and went his way, roaming the world in love and happiness.

Next morning, the rich man, Kanakapal, opened his window and looked out. What? From where? How? Who? He could not believe his eyes. There stood not far from his house, a beautiful palatial building which had not been there last evening! He called his wife to the window. She looked out and was also dumbstruck with surprise. At last she cried out, "It is our

Premchand's hut. How did it become such a palace? What magic is this?"

Before she could finish the sentence, Kanakapal was already at the front door. His wife followed him. Both of them arrived together at Premchand's house, where he was sitting and singing,

> "Hari Narayana Govinda
> Jaya Narayana Govinda
> Hari Narayana Jayanarayana
> Jai Govinda Govinda..."

As he heard the sound of approaching footsteps crunching on the newly laid gravel, Premchand got up and looked out and, seeing Kanakapal and his wife, hurried down the steps to receive his noble guests and conduct them in. Kanakapal went round the house, saw everything and heard of the mysterious blessings of the Sadhu visitor of last night.

When they were returning home, Kanakapal was very unhappy. "That Sadhu first came to us, and you were foolish enough to drive him away," accused his wife, and added, "Now, do one thing. Take the car and drive along, overtake the Mahatma who must be going on foot. Fall at his feet, and request him to allow you also three boons."

Kanakapal immediately dressed up and drove away. Not very far from the village, under a tree, the Sadhu was resting, "Hari Om, Hari Om, Hari Om." He stopped the car, ran to him and fell prostrate at his feet.

"Yesterday, Maharaj, you came first to my house, and though I used very harsh words, I was searching for the key, and before I could come down and open the front door, you had left," explained Kanakapal.

The Sadhu smiled and said, "Never mind. What do you want now?"

"Maharaj, give me also three boons as you have given Premchand," replied Kanakapal, shameless in his greed and envy.

"You have everything. You don't need them. Yet, if you desire them, you can also have three wishes, and they will all be fulfilled," declared the Sadhu. "Hari Om, Hari Om, Hari Om."

In extreme joy the greedy Kanakapal ran to his car, forgetting even to say good-bye to the Sadhu. The Sadhu smiled at the ludicrous  lunacy of one who is stung with insatiable desires. "Hari Om, Hari Om."

Kanakapal had not driven far on his way back, when the car developed engine trouble. He had not brought the tool-box with him. It was an old, old car and the battery had run down. By now the June sun was high in the sky. He pushed the car up the slope and started perspiring. The heat became unbearable. Besides, he was getting hungry. His house was yet some five kilometres away. In utter disgust and weariness he cried out, "I wish this useless car burns up completely."

All of a sudden, as if for no apparent reason, the car made an ominous sound and caught fire. On that lonely road, with no one to help him, Kanakapal screamed. The car blazed on, and in a very short time burnt down to ashes! It lay crumbled on the road. The covetous rich man knew that this was one of his wishes fulfilled!

"But then," he consoled himself, "I have two more wishes, and with them I can get the whole world if I want."

Dejectedly, he started walking home. On the way he remembered that his wife was happily sitting at home, while he was hungry and walking in the hot sun. It suddenly came out of his mouth, "I wish my house

 were on fire so that she realises how unhappy and hot I am."

It was mid-day by the time Kanakapal turned and stepped on to the road which led to his house. "What? Where is my house? What...?" He started running. As he reached the heavy gates he could smell smoke! He rushed in and dashed towards the porch! Strange! His house had been burnt to the ground. He started crying and rolling on the drive-way in agony and despair.

Kanakapal's neighbours had removed his dying wife from the burning house. She was badly burnt and scorched. They all felt pity at the tragic condition of the rich man. Seeing his wife, Kanakapal, in his sorrow exclaimed, "I wish I were blind so that I did not have to see all this tragedy." Before he had finished the sentence, he realised that all of a sudden all light had vanished from his eyes. His third wish was also fulfilled.

When Premchand heard the news, he immediately dashed to the burnt house and brought both Kanakapal and his wife into his own house. Kanakapal's wife died of burns in a week's time, in spite of the best medical attention and treatment, and Kanakapal became mentally unhinged.

Even today, the blind man sits at the gate of Premchand's house, all through the day, and in the early part of each night, and whenever he hears the sound of the approaching steps of a passer by, he asks loudly, "Is that you, O Sadhu? Please forgive me. Please give me three boons again."

If you go to Langoli Village by the Dehra Dun road, you can see Kanakapal sitting at the gate of Premchand's house, and if you approach him, he will ask loudly, "Is that you, O Sadhu? Please forgive me. Please give me three boons again."

Everybody knows that Kanakapal is mad -- but very few know how he became mad.

THE MOUSE GIRL

Once upon a time there was a small little girl mouse in a forest. She moved about freely in the forest. One day she saw a great sage sitting under a tree with eyes closed in deep meditation. The little mouse gazed at the sage in fascination. Devotion filled her tiny mind. From that day onwards the little mouse took upon herself the duty of serving the sage. With her tiny tail she would sweep the ground on which the sage would sit for meditation, sprinkle water over the place with her tiny mouth, bring flowers and fruits from the trees. The sage noticed the loving services of the tiny mouse and loved her very much.

One day as the little mouse went into the depths of the forest to bring fruits and flowers, a huge cat suddenly jumped from above the tree to pounce upon the mouse and eat her up. The mouse was terrified. Somehow she quickly ran away and entered into a rat

hole and saved herself. Till long after that she sat in the rat hole shivering and trembling with fright. After a few hours she became normal and returned to the sage. The sage was concerned about her and when he knew the reason for her absence, he pitied the mouse very much.

By his power he converted the mouse into a young girl in human form, so that in future she need not be afraid of cats and dogs. The mouse girl was very , very happy and continued to serve the sage with great love and respect.

As the years rolled by the mouse girl grew up into a beautiful young lady. It was the proper time for her marriage. The sage thought that he would find a suitable mouse boy for her and perform her marriage with him. But the mouse girl did not like it. She said, "Oh my Guru, I am now a human girl. How can I marry a mouse boy? Please allow me to marry the best one." The sage smiled and said, "All right, you choose the best bridegroom yourself. I shall surely get you married to him."

That day onwards the mouse girl was on the lookout for the best of bridegrooms. As she always lived in the forest, she had no occasion to meet any men at all except the great sage. So she did not know what best people were like. One day as she was collecting fruits and flowers in the forest, she saw a wood cutter felling the trees with an axe. When she saw how the huge tree was cut by him, she thought, "Here is the best man." Still she wanted to make sure that he was the best. She watched him for a long time as he was cutting the trees and bundling up the firewood. When he put the firewood on his head and headed for the town, she followed him.

The wood cutter went straight to the house of a rich merchant. He entered the house through the backyard, put the firewood there and came to the merchant who was sitting in the main hall in the house. He saluted the merchant and submitted respectfully, "Sir I have brought firewood for you. Please give me the money." He received the payment and went away.

When the mouse girl saw this she felt that the woodcutter was small fry and that the merchant was far superior to him. So she dropped all thoughts of marrying the woodcutter and kept watch on the merchant to see if he was the best of all. After some time, the merchant finished his work at the desk and got out of the house. There a bullock cart was waiting for him. He got into it and the cart started moving. The girl walked very fast behind the cart. The cart after some time reached the King's palace. There the cart stopped and the merchant got down and went in. The mouse girl followed him.

Inside the King was in durbar. He sat upon the throne dressed in royal robes while all others who were coming paid obeisance to him. The merchant who had a confident air till that moment became very humble in the court. He made deep obeisance to the King and stood in one corner to await the attention of the King.

When the mouse girl saw it, she knew that the merchant was not the best. She dropped all ideas of his being the possible bridegroom. She looked and looked at the King who appeared to be the best of all. But she wanted to check up thoroughly before she made up her mind to marry him. She too, stood in a corner until the durbar was over. The King rose and all arose. The King came out and sat in a palanquin. The bearers lifted it up and started walking. The mouse girl followed.

On the way, whoever saw the King, stopped and paid respects to him. The girl's heart swelled with pride at the greatness of her prospective bridegroom. Suddenly the palanquin

stopped. The mouse girl also stopped. The King got out of the palanquin, walked forward and prostrated to a sannyasin who was walking on the road. The King with great reverence touched the feet of the swami who blessed the King.

Surely, the swami was greater than the King, thought the mouse girl. She was happy that she did not make a hurried decision of marrying the King, because here was one who was better still.

Now the girl was wary. She decided not to jump to conclusions until she had met the best. She forgot all about the King and followed the sannyasin. All those who met him on the way stopped and bowed to him with great reverence. The girl was very happy to note all this.

By that time they reached a Shiva temple. The sannyasin went in. Needless to say, the mouse girl also followed. The sannyasin went near the Shiva Linga, and poured water over it. He prostrated to the Linga and sang verses in praise of Lord Shiva.

The girl was surprised. "Hey so the Linga is far superior to the sannyasin!" she thought. "Then why should I think of the sannyasin? Let me see whether any one else is greater than the Shivalinga." She waited in the temple the whole day. People came in to prostrate and pray, but the Linga remained the same. No one appeared to be greater. At nightfall all the devotees went away. Only the Linga and the mouse girl remained. In the silence of the night, out came a tiny mouse boy dancing and singing. He danced all over the place without anyone to hinder him. He even went into the sanctum sanctorum and continued his dance there. Suddenly he jumped on to the Linga and danced on its head. The Linga did not do anything at all but allowed the mouse boy to do as he pleased.

The mouse girl looked on in amazement. So, the Linga also was not the best. The mouse boy was! What a cute mouse boy! He was surely the best. He was her proper bridegroom.

The quest of the mouse girl had

ended. She went back to the sage and prostrated. The sage looked at the girl kindly and asked, "Have you discovered the best of bridegrooms?" The mouse girl bent her head shyly and nodded. She whispered, "Oh my Guru, the mouse boy in the temple is the best of all. Please make him my husband."

The sage smiled. He knew that the mouse girl would select only a mouse boy.

THE GLASS HOUSE

Kripal, the woodcutter, and his wife lived in a small village in a small hut. They were quite a happy and contented couple. The only thing was that Kripal's wife was not very neat and clean. To tell you the truth, she was really quite sloppy. Kripal was unhappy about this. It annoyed him that nothing was ever clean. He could never find anything, because nothing was ever in its right place. And he always liked things to be clean and neat and tidy. But there was not much he could do about it. When he got angry his wife always promised to be better. But she never made a real effort.

One day, Kripal went to the forest to do his work. As he was sitting down at noontime for his

lunch, he saw something shiny on the grass. He picked it up – it was a ring, a ring made of gold. How pretty it was! He put it on his finger, and as he was twisting and turning it, suddenly there was a golden glow of light, and when he looked up he saw a  beautiful fairy standing in front of him. He was quite surprised, naturally. But she was very sweet and said he should not be frightened.

As a matter of fact, he should be happy, because he had found the ring, and was therefore, entitled to a wish which she would grant. Wasn't this wonderful? He could not quite believe his eyes and his ears. He was afraid that he might not make a very wise choice. Imagine, anything he wanted! That was a big decision. He thought he had better talk this over with his wife. And the fairy consented that he could make his wish later. She told him that he must hit the ring and not think of anything but his wish, and then it would come true.

So he packed up his tools and quickly went on his way home. Oh, the possibilities! The things he could now wish for! He ran so quickly that he nearly fell over his own feet. And his mind was also running at top speed. When he was almost home and saw the hut they were living in, he suddenly thought, "I wish ... oh, no, I must be very careful with my wish!" he reminded himself.

He told his wife all about the big event of the day. They decided to sleep over the important

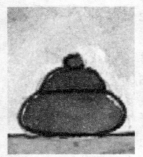

decision. Kripal thought he might as well do something until supper time and so he went to get his chisel, because he liked to carve from wood, little things like statues, images of Gods and animals.

He looked and looked, all over the place. Where on earth was his chisel? Where had his wife put it this time? Oh, this wife of his, one day she would surely drive him out of his mind with her untidiness! He got more and more angry as he searched in vain, and finally he was so angry at never being able to find anything where he had put it, that he hit his fist upon the workbench and said, "I wish this house were made of glass!"

They went to bed that night, not suspecting anything – but what should they see when they woke up the next morning? Where did all this light come from, where was the roof, why were the trees right above their eyes? Why ... yes, you guessed it. Overnight the hut had turned into a glass house. Yes, now everything could be seen – including the nosy neighbours who had gathered all around.

The wife felt very much ashamed. She crept right back under the bedcovers. Even her head went under the blankets. She did not want anyone to see her. But in the end, naturally, what could they do? Around lunchtime the neighbours went away, when Kripal and his wife got up. They had to make the best of it.

Now everybody could see what was going on in

their home. It wasn't so bad for Kripal, he was away most of the day, but the poor wife! But one day she had enough of it. She decided there was only one thing to do. Since they had to live in this glass house, she did not want to be ashamed of what the neighbours could see. So she got very busy and cleaned up the whole house, and put everything neatly where it belonged. She felt so very proud of her nice home. She even put a bowl with flowers on the table!

Kripal could not believe his eyes when he came home that night. He was so happy to see this shining, sparkling house of his. He hugged his wife and kissed her, and he hadn't done that in a long time!

And the whole village admired their beautiful house, and they all wished that they too had glass houses. But it isn't everybody who finds rings belonging to fairies, and ladies who can learn a lesson.

-- *original story adapted by Urmila, Germany*

67

YOU GET WHAT YOU GIVE

Gopal was a young boy living in a small village. As Gopal's parents were very poor, they sent him to work for a rich landlord. His duties were to look after his cattle and take them out daily into the forest for grazing and bringing them back by evening. The forest was in a valley surrounded by hills.

One day, as he was taking the cattle through the mountainous paths, he heard loud footsteps and cries calling out to the cattle. Gopal thought that there might he another cowherd like him in the valley, also looking after cattle. So he wished to meet him and make friends with him. He called out in a loud voice, "Who is there?"

In fact there was no one there. What Gopal had heard was only the echo of his own footsteps and shouts. So when he called out. "Who is there?" the echo came back from all sides. "Who is there?" Who is there?", "Who is there?". Gopal was surprised. How many boys were there in the forest? How was it that he had not met anyone of them yet?

 He cried out, "Come out and meet me." Immediately from all directions the cries came, "Come out and meet me," "Come out and meet me," "Come out and

meet me." Gopal was puzzled. He asked, "Why don't you come out and meet me?" Again the echoes came back. "Why don't you come out and meet me?" "Why don't you come out and meet me?". Now Gopal became vexed and shouted in anger, "You are a rascal."

"You are a rascal", "You are a rascal", "You are a rascal". There was a deafening series of shouts which thoroughly frightened Gopal. He quickly collected his cattle and hurried away from the forest.

Over the next few days the same thing happened again and again. Now Gopal was certain that some enemies were hiding in the forest to harm him. Supposing they all joined together and beat him, how could he escape? He could not sleep well at night, troubled by these thoughts. He wanted to stay away from work but that was not possible.

Gopal's mother observed that her son was becoming absent-minded and was unable to sleep at night. His eyes were sunken and he started looking sick. She got worried. What had happened to her boy? She asked him, "Why are you behaving so strangely? Have you quarrelled with anyone?"

Gopal burst into tears and replied amid sobs, "Mother, I don't want to go into the forest anymore. There are several wicked boys in the forest who want to hurt me."

His mother was surprised and gradually drew out the whole story from him. She understood that the boy was frightened of the echo of his own words. So she said, "Don't worry, my dear. They are not really

bad boys. They are afraid of you, just as you are afraid of them. Today when you go, you first greet them with a salutation. Then say, "You are a nice boy," and then see what happens."

Gopal had full faith in his mother. When she assured him that the boys were not bad, he overcame his fear and went to the forest with the cattle. As soon as he reached the forest valley, he said aloud, "Namaste, my friend." From all directions the echo repeated, "Namaste, my friend," Namaste, my friend," "Namaste, my friend."

Assured by this response, Gopal remembered what his mother had said. He called out, "You are a nice boy," From all directions came, "You are a nice boy," "You are a nice boy," "You are a nice boy." Gopal lost his fear. From that day onwards he uttered nice words in the valley and always got back nice words.

As he grew up into a fine, sensible young man, he realised that not only had he learnt to be unafraid, he had also learnt that the world gives back to you what you give it in the first place.

So be careful about what you give.

THAKURJI'S TOPI

A very, very rich man Sri Thakurji was. Yet, very miserly he lived. He had a disgustingly old, torn, oily, dirty topi and he would not change it. He became quite conspicuous due to his revolting appearance with his ugly old topi. The people in the bazaar even planned to raise a subscription among themselves, to make a topi fund, and present him with a new topi, and, "The rest of the fund so collected must be given as a purse to be used by Thakurji for purchasing new topies!" suggested a young man.

Though the youngsters thus planned and laughed at Thakurji behind his back, nobody dared to say anything to him directly, because he was so very rich.

He would purchase that which nobody would ever think of purchasing. Yet, his luck was such that he could make a profit even out of that rubbish. For example, some beautiful bottles were on sale. Nobody would purchase them. But Thakurji bought them all for a song. Then he bought the contents of a cellar. It contained nothing of value. But among its old bottles, casks and half-decayed, bottomless, wooden troughs and other rubbish, he found one big  jar unopened and neglected in one corner. When it was opened, to his great luck, it was found to contain a

special kind of perfume which becomes all the more precious with age and nobody knew its age! Now Thakurji decided to fill up the small bottles with the costly attar and sell them together at an unbelievably huge profit.

    This idea called for a bit of a celebration. Therefore he went to the club, and there, decided to swim and take a leisurely, luxurious bath. At the porch, he met an old friend of his, and as they were undressing, the friend said, "Thakurji, why don't you change your topi? It has become old and dirty and the talk of the town. Throw it away. Get another one. If you don't mind, even I could get one for you." Thakurji smiled and said, "This is not old enough to be thrown just yet. By next Deepavali, perhaps." And they both entered the swimming pool.

Thakurji enjoyed the cool embrace of the clean water. He rolled and ducked, slipped and splashed, again and again, in the pool. At that time, the District Judge also arrived, along with his friends and other officials. It became noisy and the swimming pool was agitated and uncomfortable. Thakurji got out quickly, dried himself and ran to the dressing room.

When he had dressed again, he could not find his old topi! "It has disappeared! Shocking!" Could it be that his friend, in his over-anxiety had thrown it away? Yes. Yes, and was he not speaking of his plan to purchase a new topi for me? That must be this solitary topi on the dressing stand. Good. Thank you all, good men - but I still do not admit that my old topi was so very old and ugly so as to be really thrown away." Taking off the rack the only topi that was there, Thakurji walked out, his head buzzing with the thoughts of how he would fill up the small bottles with the windfall attar and, within a few weeks, make the biggest profit in his business ever.

The Judge saheb got out of the swimming pool and went in to dress. When he discovered that his new topi was missing, he made very noisy complaints, and his companions, the Club Secretary and other office bearers, in deference to the high office of the Judge, started searching the place and making confused enquiries when, lo! a companion of the Judge discovered an old topi lying in one corner of the room, almost indistinguishable from the dull, dirty carpet. The moment the people saw the topi in the light, they cried out, "Surely, this is Thakurji's topi. At last he has left his topi and taken a new one!" They all seemed to be quite happy. But the Judge thundered, " His millions are not going to save him now! If he has taken my topi, the law shall deal with him." He commanded his orderlies to rush to the house of Thakurji and make a search for the lost topi.

Thakurji was in his room. He had just finished arranging the cleaned bottles all in rows, ready to receive a few drops of the attar. A knock at his door. The servant came in and  announced that some officers from the Judge's court were in the drawing room. Cursing the disturbances, he put on his new topi and walked into his spacious drawing room. Smiling, he said, "Sit down, gentlemen, what can I do for you? There is very little help I can give to anyone, as money is so tight these days..."

Thakurji suddenly stopped. He felt that the officers were looking stunned. They had angry looks. They saw Thakurji actually wearing the new topi of the Judge saheb!

In spite of the protest of Thakurji, he was hauled to the court, and in view of the fact that the accused was such a rich, but miserly member of the community, the court gave him the highest penalty of a thousand-rupee fine, and ordered confiscation of the new topi. The court, however, ordered that he must be given back his old topi. Thakurji, under loud protests, paid the fine and returned home.

He was beside himself with sorrow at the loss of money, and in sheer disgust he threw his old topi through the window into the Sabarmati river flowing behind his house. "Go you wretch! People talk of you, and now you have cost me a thousand hard earned rupees. Now you get drowned and disappear!"

The man of profit turned his attention to his work. He consoled himself that he would make up the loss by diluting the attar a little, and filling up all the bottles. Thus he started filling each small bottle with five drops less and adding water to make the bottles full.

In the meantime, the river was full. The old topi sank to the bottom and flowed down with the current. Some

fishermen had dropped their net, and the topi got caught in it. In their last haul for the evening, when the fishermen pulled up their net, there was nothing in it except a strange looking fish. They pulled it out and to their disappointment, saw that it was a piece of rag, dripping with mud. They carried it home with them and as they were going, the young fisherman who had it in his hand suddenly thought, "Why not?" and so he threw it into the window of the building he was passing by.

In the gathering gloom of the darkening dusk, the black, dirty old bundle flew in through the window, and landed on the table, upsetting all the attar bottles, smashing them all to the floor!

Thakurji was aghast. He could not

understand it. He went and picked up the rag that was the filthy cause for his stupendous loss.

And lo! What was it? His own old topi – thrown up by the river. Why?.... How?

Disappointment filled his heart. Weeping about his loss, Thakurji made a decision. He went down to the courtyard and, with a spade, he himself started digging, in his own courtyard! The neighbours became very curious. Why should Thakurji, when he had such a team of servants in his house, himself dig in his courtyard? The neighbours watched – in the dusk they could not see what it is was, but something was being buried there.

"What Thakurji buries must be money - or may be he has got a treasure there - that is it - that explains why he is so rich," thought the neighbours.

As conscientious citizens, anxious to satisfy their curiosity, they telephoned the police. The police consulted the Judge. The officer immediately ordered a posse of police to go to the spot to investigate, to open up the spot and present to the court what the rich man had concealed.

His heart loaded with sorrow, Thakurji had just finished his early dinner and was sitting morosely, brooding over the tragedies of the day, when the police started courteously enquiring whether he had dug out any treasure from under the tree! He replied defensively, "It is my own land. There is no law to stop me from digging anywhere I like, at any time, so long as it is on my land. There is nothing you can do about it." Thakurji sent them away confused.

They put a man on duty to guard the treasure and left. Next day, Thakurji was hauled to the court. The court found that his explanations were unsatisfactory. The circumstantial evidence was overwhelming. So the court ordered the digging up of the place. All that could be presented to the court was a dirty bundle. It was opened in the court and was found to be nothing but on old topi, full of river silt! It was returned to Thakurji. Holding the filthy parcel in his lap, Thakurji returned home.

He went to bed. But he could not sleep. And so he got up and harnessed his cart and drove away. He drove seven miles out of town and, looking around, he found a quiet place and huge tank. He said, "Now you go, never to return. You have brought enough troubles to me." And he threw away the bundle he had in his hand and flung it into the water. Thakurji returned home and leaving the cart and the horse in his stable, he went to bed and slept well. After all, he had finally managed to get rid of his old topi.

Next morning, everything seemed to be going smoothly. But as the day grew, the number of phone calls to the water-works department increased. From every part of the town there were screams of

complaints. There was no water in the town! The department sent its workers to find out where the trouble was. They could not find any reason. Yet, no water was reaching the town.

At last divers were sent out to the main tank. There they dived and found that the main pipe water supply to the town was choked by something. They removed it, brought it up, and lo! it was immediately recognized as Thakurji's old topi.

Again Thakurji was brought to court. As an exceptional punishment for disturbing the entire population, Thakurji was fined Rs. 25,000. With grumblings and wild protests Thakurji paid the fine and returned home. Within a few hours, a court peon brought and delivered to the servants in Thakurji's house, a parcel. When Thakurji opened it, it was found to be nothing other than his old topi!

"Why don't you leave me?," cried Thakurji, holding the topi between his fingers at eye level. "You have brought enough harm to me - you have destroyed me. You have brought great financial losses. You never leave me - you won't drown! You won't lie quietly in your grave - I threw you seven miles away; before noon next day you were back! It seems you have returned to destroy me completely! What have I done to you that you should be so revengeful towards me?

"I will now burn you - right here. I dare not go down. People may stop me." So saying, he fetched a match box. The  wet, mud-plastered topi would not catch fire easily. So in despair, he took a bundle of old newspapers, made a pyre, and burned the topi in the room. As he was sitting down and enjoying the sight of the funeral of his topi, he suddenly noticed that a huge crowd had gathered under his windows on the river banks. Bells? Sirens? Uproars?....!!

"You deserve all these and more," said Thakurji under his breath to the dying flames of the topi which was now reduced almost to ashes - when, lo! Through all the three windows of his sitting-room and bed-room, huge columns of water started streaming in, flooding the rooms, wetting everything. The dumbfounded Thakurji could not even reach the windows!

People in the neighbourhood, seeing smoke coming through his windows, had phoned the fire department to hurry to the spot. When they arrived, they saw smoke coming out of the bedroom of the palatial building. They started to do their duty in right earnest.

When everything was calm, Thakurji was really ashamed to explain what had caused the smoke in his room. The police were very suspicious. Was he burning bundles of counterfeit currency notes?

 They took away the ashes of the topi for chemical analysis. They are expecting the report... it has not yet come.

However, Thakurji has left town. They have not so far located him. The search is going on.

Poor Thakurji is now in Rishikesh as Swami Pagadidharanada. He always wears a turban now. Whenever we ask him, "Who was your Guru?" he smiles, and with reverence and devotion announces, "My teacher was a grihastha, a householder, and his revered name was Sri Topiwallah."

Elders: Everyone of us has an old topi, and like Thakurji we suffer endlessly when we try to get rid of it. This old habit or false ego, when we use it, and when it starts bringing us sorrows, we try to reject and disown it, renounce and throw it away. But like a stretched rubber band, it always rebounds back on to us. Burn it down in the fire of divine knowledge, and live in peace and joy. Be warned! You have Thakurji's old topi on your head! Get rid of it, right now!

THE THREE SUITORS

Long, long ago in a certain town, there lived a man named Krishna. He had a beautiful daughter called Susheela who was really a Susheela (talented and virtuous) in qualities as befitted her name. Many young men wanted to marry her and approached her father for her hand. Some of them had money but not good looks; some of them had neither money nor good looks. Still others who had both did not have good qualities. So he rejected most of the suitors. At last he approved three suitors who were qualified to be his son-in-law from all aspects. But whom should he choose of the three?

One day he sent for all of them together and said, "The three of you desire to marry my daughter and I like all of you. I am sure that my daughter will be happy with any one of you. I really don't know how to choose one from among you. So I shall put you all to test. The one who is the best will be chosen as my daughter's husband. What do you say?"

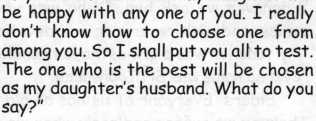

They all agreed. Then Krishna said, "I shall give you all three months' time. At the end of three months, come to me together and tell me one fine action that you have done in these months. The one who has done the best action of all will marry my daughter."

The three months were over. Krishna invited a big gathering of

elders to be present when the three young men would narrate their best deeds.

The elders would decide whose deed was the best. The women folk gathered in a corner, the elders sat on chairs, and the three suitors sat in front of them in a row.

When all were ready, Krishna turned to the suitors and asked, "Please relate to us the best deed done by you in these months."

The first suitor got up and said, "Sirs, while going through the accounts of my late father I discovered that he owed Rs. 10,000/- to one business man who is no more. His young son would not have known anything about the debt. I felt that I should discharge my father's debt even if the young man did not know it. So I showed the account to the young man and paid the whole amount to him."

The second suitor got up and said, "Sirs, last month I was passing through the forest near our town. Suddenly I heard a scuffle and a muffled scream. I ran to see what was happening. Half a dozen ruffians were manhandling a young man to loot him. Though I was alone and I had only one lathi (wooden staff) in my hand, I attacked those robbers and helped the young man. By God's grace, together we could overcame the robbers and escape safely."

The third suitor got up and said, "Sirs, one day I was passing through the range of mountains to the north of our town. There I found my sworn enemy who had done me many a bad turn, sleeping on the edge of the mountain. In his sleep he had rolled and shifted and was dangerously near the edge. Had he moved one inch more, he would have fallen into a deep valley and died. I went near him, gently woke him up and advised him to get up and sleep in a safer place."

When the three suitors had finished, Krishna turned to the elders and requested them, "Please give us your verdict. Whose deed is the best?"

The elders consulted among themselves and replied, "All the three suitors are fine men with golden qualities. Since we have to compare and contrast in order to select the best, we do so. The first suitor had been exemplary in honesty. Nowadays it is very difficult to meet with such honesty. Still, what he did was just his duty.

"The second suitor was valiant and chivalrous. He was very brave. Still, what he did was what is expected of a man. He is an ideal man.

"The third suitor is the best according to all of us, because he helped his bitter enemy. An ordinary man cannot do it. It is the Divinity within that gives such a forgiving and considerate nature.

Therefore we feel that the third suitor deserves the hand of your daughter."

All those who had gathered there applauded their decision. And on an auspicious day, Susheela was married to the noble young man with great pomp and ceremony, much to the delight of the townsfolk.

KICK THE SHELL, CLOSE YOUR EYES, SPREAD YOUR WINGS...

Ten thousand miles below the sun, in the region the modern scientists call 'space', there are two birds. One is a father bird, one is a mother bird. These birds move round and round in space, all the time, never coming down, now gliding gracefully, now flapping their wings. Sometimes chasing, sometimes calling out to each other. Since they are always in space, they are known as the 'Akash-pakshis - space birds'.

After some time, the mother bird becomes heavy with eggs. Then she lays them. Where? In space. Because they are space birds. And, because of their weight, the eggs start coming down.

Now they are not just one or two eggs. They are a whole colony of eggs. They are coming down steadily, getting ready to hatch.

When nine months have passed, the eggs have reached the warmer regions of the atmosphere, ten thousand miles above the surface of the earth.

With the heat of the sun, the shells slowly crack.

Each chick pops out its tiny head from the cracked shell. Now the mother bird, encircling in space has all the time got one eye trained on her little ones. The moment she sees them popping out their tiny fluffy heads, she swoops right down and joyfully cries out to them –

Children, children, children
Listen to me.
Kick the shell
Close your eyes
And
Spread your wings.

Round and round this colony of her young ones, she lovingly flaps, all the time calling out.

Now one chick among the rest says, "Hey! good brothers. Do not believe what she says. Have you all not noticed how cold our necks have become ever since we put them out of our warm, cosy shells? If we kick the shell and put out our whole bodies we will be cold all over."

Another chick pops its head and says, "Do not listen to this creature. She does not know what she is saying. Why, how does she know we have wings at all? What are wings, anyway?"

And thus the chicks start chirruping amongst themselves, each putting forth its own view as to why the mother bird cannot be trusted.

And all the while the mother bird, out of sheer love for her little ones, goes round and round them, calling out –

> Children, children, children,
> Listen to me.
> Kick the shell,
> Close your eyes,
> Spread your wings."

By this time there is a great deal of chattering among the chicks. Some say this is right and some say that is right.

Now, there are two chicks in the lot who are struck by the note of sincerity in the mother bird's cry. They feel, "Well maybe there is something in this. Why not give it a try? We do not understand what (the mother bird) is trying to say. But it sounds sincere enough. Why not give it a try? If we fall and sink to our doom, the others will at least know not to do the same thing. If we are all right out of the shell, they will know what to do."

So they decide to listen to the mother bird. With great courage, they kick the shell, close their eyes tight and spread their wings. And lo! Slowly, slowly, with utmost grace and beauty, the birds float in the air. They are received joyfully by the father bird who then takes them to higher realms.

The mother bird though, still hovers around the other chicks repeating her call. They are now sinking faster, till at last they have almost reached the atmospheric regions.

The father bird now sounds a note of warning. He calls down to the mother bird and warns her that she should come up before she gets sucked in the atmospheric air.

The colony slowly comes down and in the atmosphere, crumbles to little bits which appear as a faint blue mist over the early morning horizon on a wet monsoon day.